Sam's Snacks

Gerald Rose

CAMBRIDGE
UNIVERSITY PRESS

Mum and Dad were in Sam's café. Sam
wasn't feeling very well.

"AHHCHOOO!" he sneezed.

"I'm not feeling very well," he said. "I think
I'll have to close the café until I'm better."

Mum and Dad helped Sam upstairs to bed.
"You have a good rest," said Mum.
"We'll look after the café for you," said Dad.
"We'll all enjoy that."

So the next day, all the family came to
look after the café.

Gran whizzed about on her roller-skates.
"Anyone want fast food?" she asked.

Mum had fun tossing pancakes. They didn't always land in the frying-pan!

Dad burnt the sausages.

"Never mind," he said. "They'll be all right with tomato sauce."

Dan had to wash the dishes.

"I like this job," he said, "because I can blow bubbles."

There were bubbles everywhere.

But Vicky *didn't* like *her* job. The wet
plates kept slipping from her fingers and
smashing on the floor.

Some of the people didn't like their food.

"Why is there a fish-head in my soup?"
said a woman. "It's frightening my baby."
"It won't bite," said Dad.

"What are you doing?" a man shouted.
"I don't want spaghetti on my head."
"It looks very nice," said Gran.

And then . . . WHOOSH! A frying-pan
burst into flames.

"FIRE!" shouted Dad.

"CALL THE FIRE-ENGINE!" shouted Gran.

Black smoke filled the café.

"EVERYBODY OUT!" shouted Mum.

Everybody rushed outside.

"I'll phone for help," said Gran and she skated next door.

The fire-engine zoomed up.

"WHAA-WHAA, WHAA-WHAA," went the fire-engine.

Soon, a strong jet of water hissed into Sam's café.

"What about Sam?" said Mum. "He's still upstairs in bed!"

Upstairs, a window opened and Sam put his head out.

"HELP!" he yelled. "Get me down."

A fireman pulled Sam out of the window.

The next day, the family went to see
Sam in his café.

"What a mess!" said Sam. "I'll never get
it clean."

"We'll help you," said the family. "It won't take us long."

It didn't take them long.
They scrubbed and scrubbed.

And they wiped and wiped . . .
until everything was clean again.

Sam made everyone a cup of tea.
"I hope I'm never ill again," he said.
"Well if you are," said Dad, smiling,
"we're always here to help you."